JACK RIGG - MARINE ARTIST

A Brush with Shipping

A COLLECTION OF SKETCHES & PAINTINGS
BY JACK RIGG

TEXT EDITED BY MIKE ULYATT
AFTER INTERVIEWS WITH THE ARTIST

Best Wishes

J. Rigg

Published by

Richmond & Rigg Photography,
Kings Studios,
South Church Side,
HULL.
HU1 1RR

Printed by

Regal (UK) Ltd.
Crown House,
Main Street,
HULL.
HU2 0LF

Distributed by

Hutton Press Ltd.,
130, Canada Drive
Cherry Burton
Beverley
HU17 7SB
Telephone 01964 - 550573

see the complete Jack Rigg marine collection on
www.jackrigg.com

ACKNOWLEDGMENTS:

RICHMOND & RIGG PHOTOGRAPHY
ANDREW MARR INTERNATIONAL
ROYAL NATIONAL MISSION TO DEEP SEA FISHERMEN
ROYAL NATIONAL LIFEBOAT INSTITUTION
JOHN DAVIS & ASSOCIATES
G.K.D. LITHO LTD.
REGAL (UK) LTD.
CHRIS KETCHELL, (Supervisor, Local History Unit of Hull College)
ARTHUR CREDLAND (Keeper of Maritime, Hull Town Docks Museum

CONTENTS & LIST OF PAINTINGS   PAGE

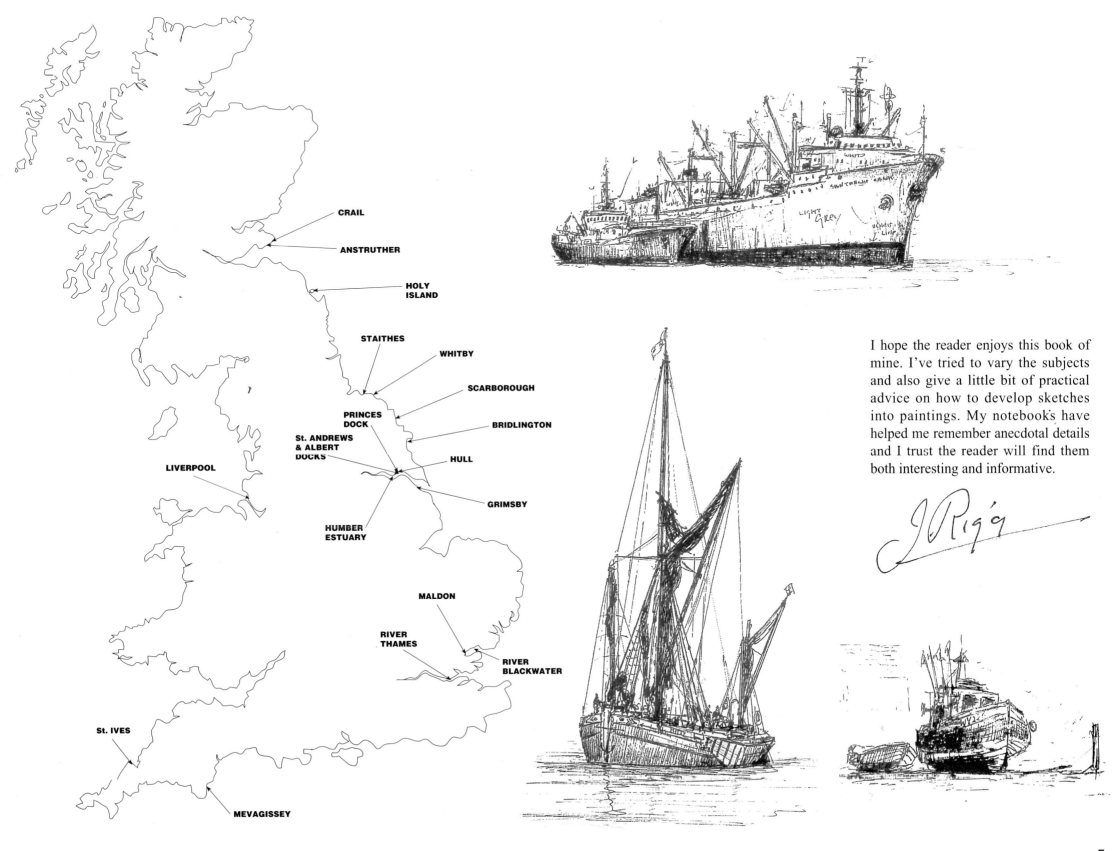

CRAIL

ANSTRUTHER

HOLY ISLAND

STAITHES

WHITBY

SCARBOROUGH

PRINCES DOCK

BRIDLINGTON

St. ANDREWS & ALBERT DOCKS

HULL

LIVERPOOL

GRIMSBY

HUMBER ESTUARY

MALDON

RIVER THAMES

RIVER BLACKWATER

St. IVES

MEVAGISSEY

I hope the reader enjoys this book of mine. I've tried to vary the subjects and also give a little bit of practical advice on how to develop sketches into paintings. My notebook's have helped me remember anecdotal details and I trust the reader will find them both interesting and informative.

6

Scarborough 1973.

ALBERT DOCK

HOLY ISLE. LINDISFARNE. JUNE 24th 1992

LOVELY SUNNY DAY AGAIN LIKE LAST YEAR

This is a general shipping scene, based around the Mersey. One would be hard put to see a scene like that today with our own ports and rivers denuded of ships and the decline of the Merchant Navy. In the early 1950s I used to take a train from Stanningley station (between Leeds and Bradford) for eight shillings (40p) return to Liverpool. What a fascinating place, it was to me, with the Cunarders leaving from the pier and the cargo ships and tugs. A trip on the ferry to Birkenhead was always the highlight of the day where there was plenty to look at, one could get really close up to the big cargo ships. All this was a bit overwhelming to take in at once and my only regret is that I did not have a camera to record it at all. This is a painting based on some happy memories of the area. I deliberately made the background hazy and smoky to draw more attention to the liner.

I sketched this scene while on holiday in the Spring of 1994. We were staying with friends, in fact my wife Shirley's former teaching tutor. Harbour scenes and fishing boats have always interested me. This picture is not strictly accurate as I added some of my own ideas to give the scene better composition. When translated, the name of the fishing boat in the foreground, the SS 579 *La Mouetta*, means "The Seagull".

I have always found Cornwall very inspiring with its own particular types of fishing boat and have spent many happy hours sketching them. I also have spent a while in places such as Newlyn where Stanhope Farber lived last century and had his group, also Falmouth, Coverack and Penzance.

This was another painting I started while I was on holiday in the area in 1964 with my wife Shirley and sons Michael and Ian. They were happy enough to play on the beach while I set up my easel opposite the action. I also made notes on my sketch pad of the various colours of the boats and the buildings and whether the boats were clinker or carvel built. I always use a ruler to make sure I get the masts and rigging straight, an important point in my opinion. Twice we went down to Mevagissey as I found such a lot to sketch there, most of which eventually became paintings. It was while staying in Mevagissey I had a sketching trip to Fowey which I find one of the most Cornish of them all. Here I met the late Mr Leo Walmsley, the Yorkshire author from Robin Hoods Bay. Another interesting trip was to Par and Charlestown, a small working harbour. I was lucky to see a coaster entering the very narrow harbour entrance. It was manoeuvred through with a series of hawsers.

I sailed on the Thames Sailing Barge *Reminder* for twelve consecutive years, sometimes as a crew member and sometimes just to sketch. They were the "work horses" of the Thames estuary and cost a fortune to restore and sail again. My most memorable trip was from St. Katherine's Dock near Tower Bridge to Maldon in Essex, my favourite area for sketching – lots of sky and calm waters. Then there was lots of shipping to interest me – not so much nowadays. The owner of *Reminder* held an Open Art Exhibition annually on board which proved quite successful. All this would have been in the 1970s. To sail in a Barge Match and observe these beautiful craft at close quarters with their huge sail erected is a sight to see. *Reminder* is a steel barge and was built at Mistley for T. W. Horlock in 1929. These barges were christened Ironpots as opposed to the older ones which were all built of wood. The older wooden barges have the most beautifully decorated sterns and massive heavy rudders; lacking on the Ironpots, although they are still imposing vessels. S.B. *Reminder* had a very successful career in her days as a racing barge, frequently coming first in her class. Two of the best books on barges are "Sailing Barges" by the late Mr Frank G. G. Carr and "Spritsail Barges of Thames and Medway" by Edgar J. March. Both classics.

Sailing Barge *Dawn* being towed into Maldon after the Blackwater Barge Match in 1977.

Sailing barge *Dawn* was originally a stackie barge used for carrying hay from outlying farms to London. London at that time not being motorised, an enormous amount of hay was required to feed the horses. This was usually loaded up in the creeks and small ports in East Anglia and transported down the Thames to London. Having studied old photographs of the stackie barges loaded up I never cease to wonder how on earth the men (sometimes a man and a boy) could manoeuvre their barge down the coast and into the Thames Estuary and into the docks at a period when the river was thick with ships of every description. I sailed in the Blackwater match a couple of times; the Medway match twice; the Colne match once; and the Pin Mill match a few times; always purely as a spectator to get ideas for paintings. I have many happy memories of the East Anglian rivers, the Blackwater, Thames, Medway, Crouch, Colne, Orwell and the one to Oxford. My firm favourite was the Orwell up to Ipswich. After the Pin Mill barge matches, there was always a sociable evening in the Butt & Oyster and I have to admit once drinking too much of their very delightful local cider one evening after a full day's racing. A guiding hand back to the barge was very welcome.

This was originally an idea for a 26" x 18" canvas as a summer scene, but the Royal National Mission to Deep Sea Fishermen approached me in 1988 with a request for a Christmas Card design – so I changed it to a winter scene. It's quite easy to alter an oil painting. I just put in snow on the roofs of all the buildings and made the sky a bit more wintry. I also outlined the boats in white to give an impression of snow and frost and I added icy water to give the whole painting a feeling of mid-winter. I have to admit Winter landscapes are my favourite subjects. I think the Mission sold over 180,000 cards and so it was all worthwhile. I was delighted to help them raise money to fund their very worthwhile work among fishing communities. In the painting, when finished, I had painted the sun setting on the right of the church, so as to have reflections in the water to balance the picture up. I had visited Maldon lots of times but on reflection could not remember the setting sun being there. As I knew this painting was going to be reproduced as an Xmas card and would be seen by a lot of people including the locals, I thought I had better check up and get it right. Sure enough I was wrong and had to do with a patch of light cloud. I was told by a local man who was interested in painting, that many artists had made that mistake before. Maldon being a small port and interesting old town has always attracted artists, particularly Hythe Quay with its Sailing Barges.

J. RIGG 1996

SIREN   SKETCHEN   LAID   UP   AT   MALDON   Essex 1988

This painting was inspired by actually seeing the two craft passing off the Essex Coast. These were observed from the Sailing Barge *Reminder*. Later in 1988 I had the chance to see and sketch the *Siren* when she was laid up at Maldon. *Thallata* is one of the bigger barges, being "Mulie Rigged" that is with the mizzen set on a gaff and boom. I had a chance to have a good look at her and sketch this very smart craft when I was in Mistley up the River Stour. *Thallata* is owned by the East Coast Sail Trust and acts as a seagoing working holiday for young people. You have to be careful when painting the sea. I like to make sure the oils are dry before adding any lighter colours including bow waves etc. But that is just my method; Many artists paint wet on wet with excellent results.

SAILING BARGE "KITTY." MALDON AUG 1976

There was plenty of time to sketch on this trip when the Thames Sailing barge *Kitty* was becalmed on the River Blackwater in August 1977. I remember our skipper playing his guitar to entertain us. A crew of 14 was usually on a barge trip including the skipper, mate and cook. A painting can take two or three days to dry if the weather is fine, up to five days if it's cold or there is damp in the air. I put in all the rigging when the paint is dry. I prefer a rough surface to paint on – a flax canvas suits me down to the ground, but they are expensive to buy. Sometimes the sky and sea change moods very rapidly so it is important to capture your image quickly if you are painting on location, which I prefer – it's easier to refer to details rather than look up my sketch notes. It is also best, of course, for establishing the basic colour references, although these do get firmly engraved in my mind's eye. When I'm finishing a painting, even from sketch notes, the colours come back – sometimes many years later. So if I've written "blue" on, say, a ship's hull I'll know exactly what blue it was. I love painting misty early morning or early evening pictures like this one is. I tend to try and finish the sky and background first, but keeping a rough picture of the main subject all throughout. I usually find with backgrounds like this, with light breaking through the mist that at least three applications are necessary. Each must be left to dry before adding the light source and finishing the main subject in the picture.

Grimsby

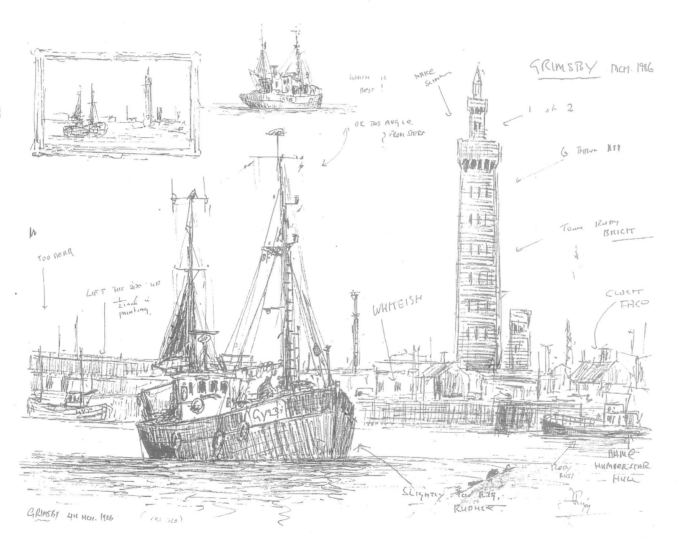

I just wanted to draw this scene. I parked the car right next to the brick tower which I think was used to hydraulically open the lock gates. Skylines have always interested me – I don't like insipid skies and prefer to paint mine with plenty of dramatic clouds. One day I was looking at my original painting, which was on display in the windows of the Hull Telephone Company in Carr Lane, and I got into conversation with a gentleman who was taking a particular interest in the painting. It turned out he had once been the skipper of the *Humber Star* which is the vessel on the right of the picture. Having studied old photographs of Grimsby in its hey day as a fishing port crammed with trawlers, I felt my painting seemed a bit desolate and empty. The whole scene around this area has changed dramatically since I sketched the scene in March 1986.

Humber Keel

The Humber Keel *Comrade* was built as the *Wanda* at Warrens Shipyard at New Holland in 1923 and was acquired by the Humber Keel and Sloop Preservation Society from Capt Fred Schofield on 16 December 1974. She was traditionally restored and sailed again on 14 August 1976. The Society charters *Comrade* out most weekends from April to September each year. Their Sailing Commodore Colin Screeton is an acquaintance of mine. While not as well known as the Thames Sailing barges, keels certainly sailed in profusion on the River Humber and associated waterways up to the 1930's. Barges of all types have always interested me, having been born not far from the Leeds & Liverpool canal. The barges that used to be a regular sight pre-war have virtually disappeared. What a wonderful subject these made.

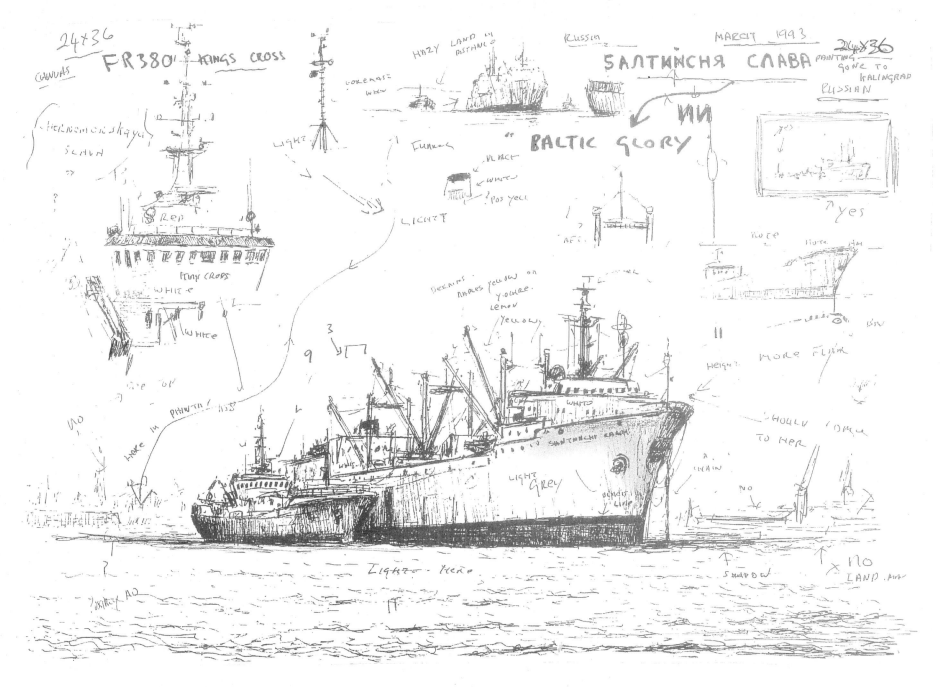

I was commissioned by Andrew Marr International, Hull, to paint the Балтийская Слава (*Baltic Glory*) in 1993 with the FR380 *Kings Cross* alongside. This particular commission was quite difficult and there was lots of technical detail to make the painting authentic. I made sure I had lots of photographs and made plenty of sketches so I was confident I had captured the scene in detail and I was very pleased with the finished work. The 40" x 30" framed colour print hangs in the offices of Andrew Marr International and the original framed canvas was sent to Kalingrad as a present from the Company to cement a new business venture.

This was based on a drawing I sketched on June 24, 1971. A friend of mine sold conveying systems and I joined him on a visit to Hull. We presented ourselves to the policeman on duty at the dock gates who was really interested in what I intended to do and he came to look at my progress several times during the four or five hours I spent sketching while I waited for my friend to finish his sales meetings. I eventually completed the painting in 1994. The trawlers are J. Marr and Son's *Brucella* and the Ross Group's (later British United Trawlers) *Ross Orion* – H235." I will always remember the intense activity going on that day at St. Andrew's Dock – now all sadly gone. It was in 1994 while travelling on the Clive Sullivan Way past the almost filled-in St. Andrew's Dock, that I noticed the bit of stone jetty still standing, which seemed to remind me of something. On digging out my old sketches, done that day together with a black and white snapshot I had taken, I recalled that day 23 years before.

Arctic Corsair coming home to Albert Dock

This painting came about quite accidentally. I had received a commission to paint a picture of the STS *Sir Winston Churchill* and was waiting for her to berth at 2 p.m. on 18 August 1986 at the Albert Dock, Hull. She had an all-girl crew that trip and quite a few of the parents were waiting for her to arrive. They were all getting rather worried when by six p.m. there was no sight of the *Sir Winston Churchill*. We were then informed that due to delays she would not arrive till between 6-7 a.m. next morning. I was down at the dock next morning before six a.m. But the first ship to arrive was the Boyd Line sidewinder trawler *Arctic Corsair* – hence the painting. The *Sir Winston Churchill* did berth an hour later. My commission of her was rejected as the buyers wanted her in full sail and sunshine. I had captured her with all sails furled on a misty dull morning. The *Arctic Corsair* has now been restored to her original condition and there are plans to give her a permanent mooring in the port.

IDEA FOR 30X18 CANVAS OLD HULL FROM PRINCES DOCK.   RECONSTRUCTION FROM OLD PHOTOGRAPH.

Hull in its heyday. There's a lot of history in this painting – St. John's Church, the Wilberforce monument and the Dock Offices in the background with the Dock itself full of Humber Keels and Sloops. This dock was originally known as the Junction Dock when it linked the Humber and Queens Docks in 1829. Trade in the Dock was mainly German, Dutch and coasters. The Wilberforce monument was moved to the east end of the Queens Gardens after the Queen's Dock itself was filled in during the 1930's. I based the whole scene on old photographs, but I was taken to task by a seaman over the painting. He gleefully pointed out that the funnel on the liner showed the Harrison Line colours when that particular shipping company never used the Princes's Dock. He said the colours should have been the red and black of the Ellerman Wilson Line. I had to apologise, of course! One cannot be too careful when researching for a period in a painting, and it taught me a lesson to be more

When I first came to Hull in 1947, there were many bomb-damaged sites in Hull city centre. It always fascinated me to see the trawlers being fitted out or repaired in the north-west corner of this Dock, near to where the actress Maureen Lipman's father kept a tailors shop for many years. This whole area has changed – the Town Docks Offices have been converted into the Town Docks Museum and a shopping centre, Princes's Quay, occupies half of the dock. I painted the background based on old photographs, then the water and then the shipping – that's my normal procedure, and it works for me.

What a pleasant scene this is on a 1980s bright sunny day. Hull Marina was completed in the early 1980s from the disused Humber Dock and is very well situated in the city centre. The lightship itself was built by Cook, Welton and Gemmell of Beverley in 1954 for the British Transport Docks Board and it was stationed at the mouth of the River Humber with a crew of eight on board on a shift basis. The Spurn Lightship was withdrawn from service in 1975 and was taken over by Hull City Council, restored and berthed in the Marina in 1986. The Lightship is now open to the public. Lightships have always held great interest for me. In 1981, while on a sailing barge trip, we anchored one day off Parkstone Quay, near Harwich. Quite a few lightships were riding at anchor prior to being laid up and replaced by the unmanned type, which I thought by comparison very ugly things. As we were there for a whole day, I had ample time to sketch and study these ships with their bright red hulls and white superstructure.

This stretch of the river near to North Bridge and Drypool Bridge used to be a favourite area of mine – full of all sorts of working boats and barges and the quaysides were always bustling with activity. Rank's Clarence Flour Mills, the dry docks, ship-building yards, oil mills, coasters, barges, tankers, pleasure boats, cranes, and buildings – I was really spoilt for choice on what to sketch. I used to set up my easel on a Sunday evening when it was a bit quieter and my sketch book was full of drawings made during the week. I completed this painting in 1982. I have always preferred to stand up when I'm painting because I can step back and take a wider view of my subject matter and my painting. This area was badly damaged during the bombing of Hull in the war. Studying old photographs of the River Hull pre-war it looked a place full of ships and interest. While realising this must have been good from an artists point of view, conditions must have been pretty hard for one working there.

There are always plenty of small trawlers and pleasure craft to sketch in Bridlington Harbour – it always seems to be busy and the background is ideal with so many different styles and heights of the buildings in the immediate area. Here the Grimsby small trawler GY 226 dominates the scene at low tide – proportions are very important to a painting and this one is a good example. I've included plenty of detail with lobster pots on the old wooden harbour decking, mooring ropes and a hazy background. I completed this painting in 1992 from sketches I had made a few years before.

Mr Cook of Bridlington Harbour Trawler Co., commissioned me to paint PO53 *Galatea*. I had originally sketched the trawler some years earlier while she was undergoing repairs in Whitby Shipyard. I received a telephone call one morning telling me the *Galatea* was due in Bridlington Harbour that afternoon, so I drove across from Leeds with my wife Shirley. We parked the car and she stayed on one side of the harbour wall with a pair of binoculars and I positioned myself down on the steps across the harbour mouth. Shirley shouted across when the *Galatea* came into view after a two hour wait. At the precise moment when the *Galatea* was entering the harbour a yacht sailing out nearly obscured her from my view, but I managed to get my photograph. When she had tied up I was able to do some drawings of the deck house and various other bits and pieces which are essential for a painting of this nature. One of my pictures of the *Galatea* was used on the front cover of the Royal Mission To Deep Sea Fisherman's Magazine "Toilers of the Deep."

The red roofed houses tumbling down the steep road to the sea make this a favourite scene for many artists and photographers, full of character. I've always found the Yorkshire coble very difficult to sketch. The traditional bonnet worn by the women in the village was made from a yard of cotton material, cut into a nine-piece pattern, tied at the back with a bow and had a double crown and a double pleated frill at the front, some three inches wide. It protected the women's hair as they helped the fisherfolk unload their catches. These bonnets are rarely seen nowadays. Staithes was also well-known for the famous "Staithes Group of Artists" to which Dame Laura Knight belonged.

The Grimsby Trawler GY237 entering Scarborough Harbour early one morning in 1991. This is another favourite area of mine for sketching. You have to make sure all rigging, cabin and crew details are correct, otherwise some fishermen will put you right! The Grand Hotel dominates Scarborough's South Bay. Overlooking the Spa, the hotel was designed by Hull architect Cuthbert Brodrick and was built between 1862 and 1867. It was based on the American pattern of a suite of large public rooms combined with bedrooms and private sitting rooms. I think there are around 300 bedrooms and the hotel is now owned by Butlins. This interesting and majestic building always forms a good backdrop for a painting of Scarborough. Trying to depict this in a misty way is always very trying, and I can't remember the number of times I have felt like taking the painting off the easel and doing a war dance on it.

Low Tide, Scarborough

LOW TIDE SCARBOROUGH   USE FOR PAINTING.

There are usually three stages to my work – the sketch, outline painting and completing the painting after which I varnish it when all the oils are dry. I love to go to Scarborough on a spring tide at low water. One can usually get to see a different aspect of the harbour giving one new ideas for future paintings. I lowered the lines of the blue trawler as they were too high on my original painting, which was finished in 1987. Using a palette knife (a spatula with a thin flexible blade) allows me to work the background in quickly.

SCARBOROUGH   V.COLE

SCARBOROUGH 1985. LOW TIDE

50

J.RIGG 1987

My idea for this was a 20" x 30" canvas. I lowered the land mass in the background to give much more emphasis to dark angry sky. I've often been out to sea on small trawlers, so I could get a better idea of coastlines, and I once ended up as a deckhand, hauling up lobster and crab pots. Fishermen are a special breed of men and I've every admiration for them as they face the elements of wind and sea so regularly

My first visit to Scarborough was on a day trip by charabanc in 1932 and I remember seeing Dutch fishing boats in the harbour and the crew with corduroys and clogs. I received my calling up papers for Service in the Royal Navy while I was on holiday here in 1945. I made sketches for this painting in 1973, using the castle in the background, also sketches for this painting were completed in the harbour of the fishing boat the *Caroline* SH129. This was a very interesting fishing boat having lots of character with her sturdy masts and red mizzen sail. Grey skies always have fascinated me, especially when there are at least half a dozen shades of grey in the sky at the same time. Always interesting trying Blue black and Naples yellow, Paynes grey, Davy's grey, and of course various mixtures of blue and red.

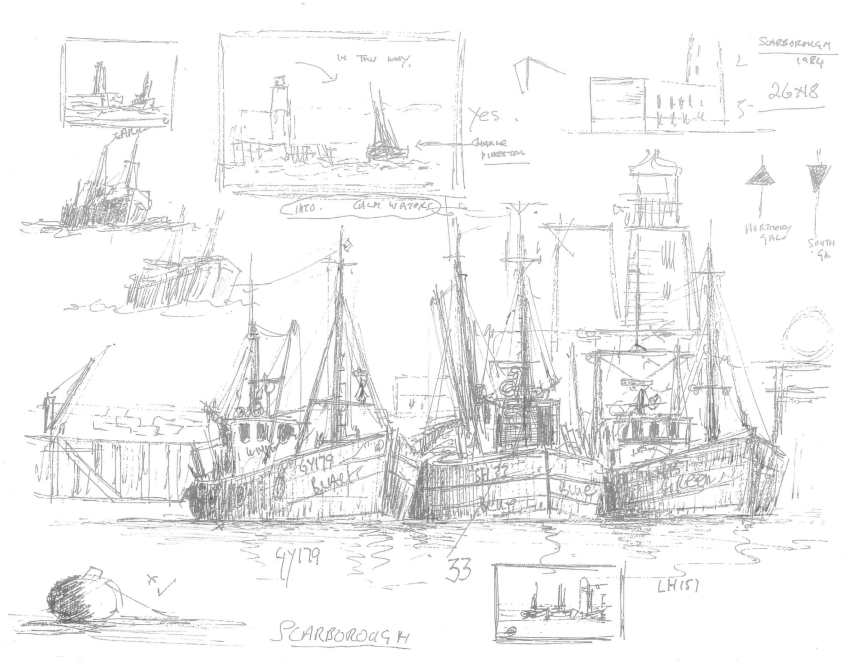

I made quite a few sketches for this painting in the Summer of 1984 with the lighthouse behind the trawlers. Scarborough has many happy memories for me and the harbour has always had many interesting craft moored which I have sketched over the years.

J.RIGG 1988

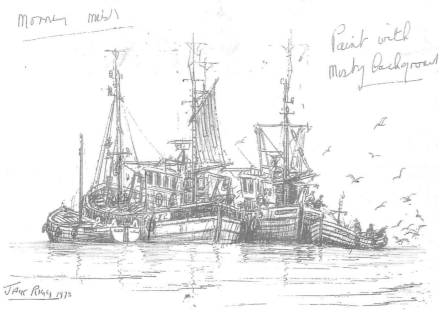

Morning mist

Paint with Misty Background

I tried to give this painting a bit more atmosphere than usual by featuring early morning mist which is difficult to convey but always fascinating with the rising sun trying to break through the clouds. I think it gives the painting a 'silent' quality. One could hire a rowing boat for as long as one wanted at both Bridlington and Whitby. It enabled one to get a really good view of the harbour craft for sketching or photography. I have always thought it is more interesting viewing any craft from the deck of a small boat. Somehow I could never get enthusiastic for aerial views. Although I can recollect spending hours rowing at Whitby and Bridlington, I cannot remember Scarborough having the same facilities.

My eldest son Michael lived in Whitby for 10 years. I was able to observe the seas and fishing boats in many types of weather as I accompanied my son who regularly rowed out to and around the Whitby Buoy in his 11ft. rowing boat. He was training for his 160 mile single handed row to Great Yarmouth which he achieved in seven days of almost non-stop rowing. Michael in 1980, a 25-year-old 3rd Officer in the Merchant Navy left Whitby in a force 6 gale. He carried flares, a life jacket, a two-way radio and enough food and water for two weeks. He plotted his course with the aid of a sextant and compass and kept in daily contact with the coastguard stations via passing ships to give them his position. It was with great relief we were telephoned of his safe arrival by the Yarmouth coastguard. Actually viewing the pier extensions from a rowing boat, looking into the harbour, has given me many ideas and inspirations for paintings in the past.

Ready To Sail, Whitby Harbour

WHITBY 1973

I sketched plenty of background details of Whitby west side looking inland with the swing bridge closed to shipping and I made sure the tiles, sloping roofs, steps and shops were drawn in fine detail. The three trawlers were then sketched in and once again the sky completes the painting. I could nearly paint Whitby from memory, I've spent so much time there. During the 1960's many weekends were spent at a friend's house in nearby Robin Hood's Bay, while the family went shopping in Whitby on a Saturday, I spent the day sketching. Most of the fishing boats at that time were open decked, and looked very attractive. The white whaleback now seems to be a feature of all fishing boats and no doubt must be a great asset for the fishermen themselves in bad weather

I was sketching this scene at the bottom of the harbour steps at low tide, trying to get the trawlers mizzen sail details correct, when the lifeboat came close in and its wash half covered me. As I can't swim, the experience came as a great shock, but I am sure that the crew were having a joke at my expense.

Whitby lifeboat in action
Sunday A.M. October 1980
44 WAVENY

44-012

W.H. LIGHTS   42-02?

SMOKE
Hen

CITY OF SHEFFIELD

TROLLEY

no au Stern

Idea for Whitby lifeboat   20x30

44-012

RED BAW
DEEP BLUE
WHITE
RED

RNLI. CITY OF SHEFFIELD

CITY OF SHEFFIELD

47-02?

now whitby lifeboat
Whitby Harbour
1990

The *City of Sheffield* lifeboat helping a trawler in difficulties off Whitby. I have painted quite a few pictures of the town's two previous lifeboats. The *Mary Ann Hepworth* was a very good subject in the 1960's. It is good to see it is still sailing from Whitby Harbour taking visitors for a trip round the Buoy and it featured in a recent Yorkshire Television documentary. I am a "Shoreline" member of the Royal National Lifeboat Association and exhibit annually in the RNLI Art Exhibition in Whitby.

I based this painting on sketches I made when I went out a couple of times on a fishing boat (I was terribly seasick once!) and also based on a lifeboat that was stationed in Whitby for a period while the regular one which is normally on station was away having an overhaul. It was the combination of two separate drawings used to depict something that might have happened. I have tried to portray a stormy day. and wanted the sky to give an impression of danger. For 25 years I have been a member of the Fylingdales Group of Artists. It was formed in the 1920's and membership is by invitation only. We have 22 members at any one time and meet twice a year with an annual exhibition in Pannett Park, Whitby. When exhibited at the Fylingdales exhibition, the picture was bought by a former owner of the WY12.

In October 1980, a man and his son-in-law got into difficulties near the harbour mouth and their small boat overturned in rough seas. The son-in-law was rescued by the lifeboat, but the man's body was never found. I have always found lifeboats to be inspiring and when I saw it in action that morning with Peter Thompson at the helm, I was full of admiration for the men who so often risk their own lives to help others and venture out in the most appalling weather.

I stayed with an artist friend and spent days with him sketching around Bamburgh and Seahouses in the summer of 1992. The weather was beautiful and when the tides were favourable we visited Holy Island. I enjoyed capturing a different type of seascape. The upended boats we found to be so interesting, some even having a window and door fitted. One proved very convenient for us on a sketching trip, as we were able to shelter from a very cutting wind and work in comfort sat on old fish boxes. A trip to Seahouses wasn't as rewarding as I had not been sketching there since the 1960's. All the old type fishing boats seemed to have been replaced by a very modern version though it still held some very interesting large cobles. Another trip out to Eyemouth proved fruitful, also to Burnmouth down the steep winding road. Northumberland offers plenty of scope for anybody looking for something new and different to sketch or paint.

This sketch was based on Anstruther, but the scene could well be repeated anywhere along Britain's coast where fishing communities exist – families waiting and praying for the safe return of their menfolk when bad weather threatened. I know from experience the tremendous work the Royal National Mission to Deep Sea Fishermen do when tragedy strikes at sea.

WHITE

WHITE

SANDY.

SANR

WALL

CRAIL

SKETCH FOR SCOTTISH HARBOUR

The relief when the fishing fleet returned home safely to port must have been enormous among the fishermen's families and their local community. I was stationed in Arbroath for a year in 1946 during my Royal Navy service and had ample time to sketch along the east coast of Scotland, especially at Crail. A fellow artist criticised this harbour scene, saying it was too cluttered on the left of the picture and I'm sure he's right. Constructive criticism has never bothered me, in fact, I always welcome it, you're never too old to learn. Sometimes the most constructive criticism I have learned from is just showing a picture to someone and asking for comments as to what they think of it. I get some very interesting replies. By painting the two buildings white, I've tried to draw attention to the buildings in the background as well as the boats in the harbour.

J.RIGG

WHITBY TUG

WV103 Rosie

SAILING BARGE "KITTY."   MALDON AUG 197

STAITHES. 1928.

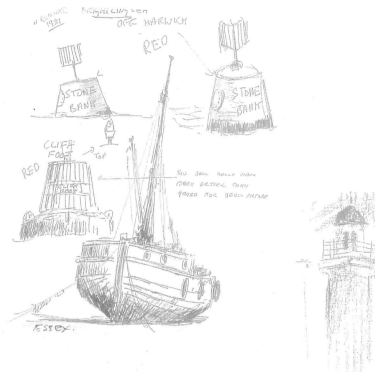

H. ROBINSON
1981
BRIGHTLINGSEA
OFF HARWICH

RED

STONE BANK

STONE BANK

CLIFF FOOT
TOP

RED

CLIFF FOOT

THIS BOUY WOULD HAVE
BEEN BETTER THAN
WAVED FOR YOUR PICTURE

ESSEX.

LINE

H 424

Idea for Cover Sketch Harbour